Backyard Sustainability in the Goldfields

~ Jared and Josh Campbell ~

the book incubator

Sometimes we hang out in veggie gardens or with the chooks.

Published by The Book Incubator:, May 2020
Book layout and design The Book Incubator

www.bookincubator.com.au

Bunbury, Western Australia

Backyard Sustainability in the Goldfields © Jared Campbell, and Josh Campbell, 2020
Soft Cover ISBN: 978-0-6487471-1-6
Hard cover ISBN: 978-0-6487471-0-9

This project is proudly sponsored by

Hi our names are Josh and Jared Campbell and we want to make a difference in the world. We live in the Goldfields of Western Australia. This book is all about how we can be sustainable in our own homes. People think to make a difference you have to think large scale ideas like solar farms. Everyone could be making a massive difference right in your own home. If we were all sustainable in our backyards, we could achieve so much more than one person ever could!

From little things big things grow!

~Jared & Josh ~

Contents Page

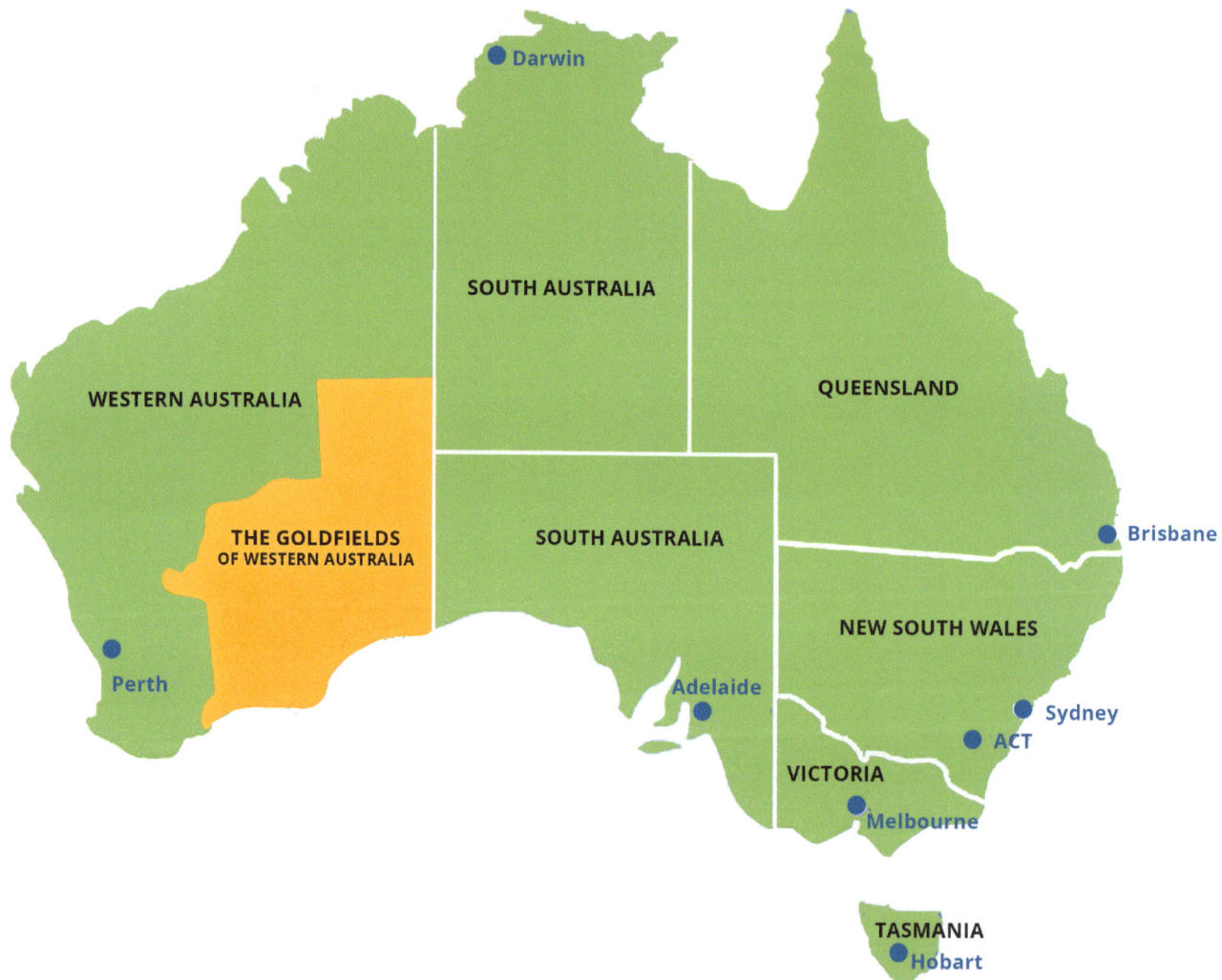

WESTERN AUSTRALIA

THE GOLDFIELDS
OF WESTERN AUSTRALIA

SOUTH AUSTRALIA

SOUTH AUSTRALIA

QUEENSLAND

NEW SOUTH WALES

VICTORIA

TASMANIA

Darwin

Perth

Adelaide

Brisbane

Sydney

ACT

Melbourne

Hobart

INTRODUCTION

Sustainability can be defined by the ability to be maintained at a certain rate or level or avoidance of the depletion of natural resources in order to maintain an ecological balance.("How sustainable is sustainability? - Oxford College of Procurement and Supply", n.d.).

Most people are aware that the Earth's resources are not infinite and that our population is increasing dramatically. This means that at some time in the future we will run out of resources that we need to survive like fuel, fresh water and building materials like iron ore. People are becoming more aware that we need to recycle what we use, use less of the resources we are running out of and think more about the environmental future of our planet.

Big companies, governments and scientific groups are discussing and implementing strategies to become more environmentally sustainable. Like building solar and wind farms to produce the energy we need instead of burning fossil fuels like coal. As well as building desalination plants to provide fresh drinking water from sea water, instead of using land sources of fresh water which has a large ecological impact on the land environment.

In our home, we try to be sustainable in many ways, but we are one of millions of households across Australia and one of billions in the World. On our own, we make very little difference, but if lots of households followed the same sustainable way of thinking, we can make a difference.

The following chapters describe how we are trying to be sustainable in our own backyard. Most of the photographs are of our backyard. We live in the Goldfields Region of Western Australia and you may not be able to do some of the things we describe, but we hope we can give you some new ideas and encouragement to be more sustainable at home.

WAYS TO BE WATER WISE

CONNECT YOUR GUTTERING TO WATER TANKS TO STORE WATER FOR DRINKING OR WATERING YOUR GARDEN

WHY: Rain falls freely from the sky. It soaks into the ground and runs off roofs into gutters and away from the house or shed. By storing the rainwater from gutters, you can have a lot of spare water to use on gardens or animals. You could also drink it if it is filtered properly. Some people even use stored water for a greywater system, which is using it for toilet water etc.

HOW: You can connect the guttering from the roof of your house, carport and sheds to go into watertanks to be stored. The size of your water tank will depend on your budget, the size of your backyard or its purpose.

IF YOUR HOUSE HAS A SLOPE, USE IT TO COLLECT RAINWATER RUNOFF INTO GARDENS

WHY: Rain soaks into the ground but excess rainfall can be collected to soak in where it is needed, instead of running down the road and into drains. Sometimes only a little bit of rain will fall, but by diverting the water an area can receive quite a bit.

HOW: We divert rainwater from the top of our backyard through shallow channels to our fruit tree area. Here there are mounds of dirt around the base of each tree to collect the runoff and allow the water to soak in. Our native garden at the front of our house collects surface runoff from the driveway and front gutters.

WATER

In Australia, people are well aware that the most precious resource we have is fresh water. Australia is a very dry continent with large areas of desert and low rainfall. This provides large challenges for agriculture, industry and places where people can live.

Being water wise is important in the Goldfields because this Region has a low rainfall of around 260mm per year. Most of the Goldfields Region is supplied with water from Mundaring Weir through CY O'Connor's famous pipeline. The supply to the Weir is limited by Perth's rainfall.

More remote areas in the Goldfields Region collect their water from rainfall, underground aquifers and desalinisation plants.

WAYS TO BE WATER WISE

USE DRIP RETICULATION INSTEAD OF SPRAYING

WHY: Drip reticulation delivers the water straight to the base of the plants and the root system. There is very little water lost to evaporation or wetting the ground where there is no plant.

HOW: Make sure your reticulation is the drip type and not fine spraying sprinklers. We use sprinkler heads that can vary the flow of water and place them on flexible hose to move the sprinkler to where it is needed.

MULCH YOUR GARDEN TO REDUCE WATER LOSS AND KEEP THE GROUND COOL

WHY: Mulching provides a barrier between the ground and the air. It shades the ground preventing it from getting very hot in summer and helps reduce evaporation from the soil.

HOW: More common mulches include chopped up waste plant material such as wood, branches and bark. We use horse manure because it is free from our horses and dries out leaving a layer of finely chopped plant material.

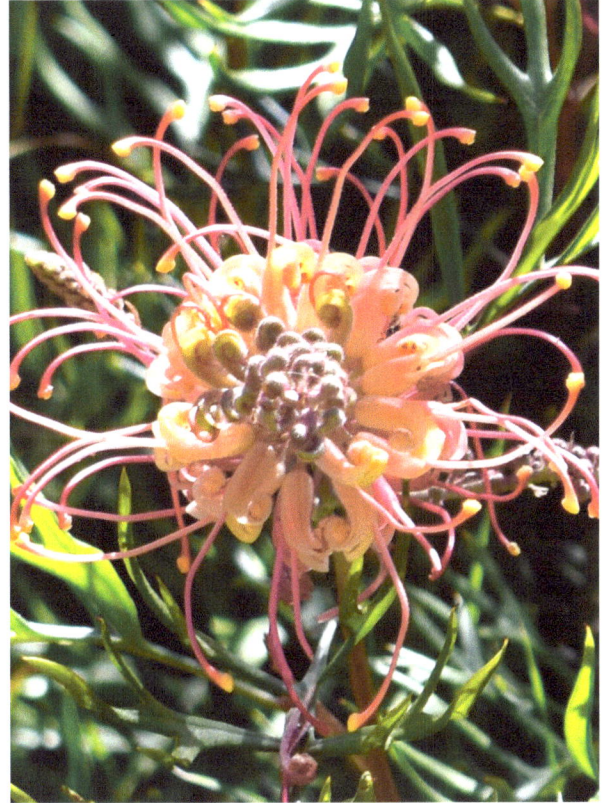

PLANT NATIVE PLANTS THAT HAVE ADAPTED TO A LOW RAINFALL CLIMATE

WHY: Plants that are native to the area you live are already used to the climate of your area. They are found there because they are able to survive the rainfall of that area.

HOW: The Goldfields region has a rich diversity of native plants from Eucalyptus trees to smaller Eremophila shrubs that are naturally drought tolerant. Our front yard consists of Eucalyptus trees that shade smaller shrubs such as Grevilleas, Hakeas and a wide variety of Eremophilas While not all are endemic to the Goldfields they are all drought tolerant. With runoff from when it rains, horse manure mulching and drip reticulation, we water the front yard very little.

ENERGY

Goldfields power comes from Perth via Western Power's Transition Line. Although power comes from Perth, Kalgoorlie has three gas turbine units that provide backup power for peak periods or emergencies. The majority of our power is produced using fossil fuels, which is unsustainable, so we should limit our usage of these fuels and invest in more renewable power such as solar and wind.

Photo by Pexels on Pixabay

TURN LIGHTS OFF WHEN YOU DON'T NEED THEM

WHY: Using the lights uses power. Every little bit of energy conservation adds up over time, especially if we all do it together.

HOW: If we used 5c less of power each day by turning off the lights we don't use, that would equal $18.25 in savings a year! And that is one house – imagine if we all did it together??!! 1,000 houses doing this would save $18,250 a year!! That equals a lot of power that didn't need to be generated.

USE ENERGY EFFICIENT LIGHT BULBS

WHY: Energy efficient light bulbs use less energy because they don't produce so much waste heat.

HOW: When you replace the light bulbs in your house, check that they are energy efficient where possible.

WAYS TO BE ENERGY EFFICIENT

LOOK FOR HOUSEHOLD ITEMS WITH A HIGH ENERGY EFFICIENCY RATING

WHY: Energy efficient household items such as dryers, fridges and TVs use less energy than normal items. Not only do they save power, but they save you money.

HOW: If we need a new household item, we try to find the best energy rating. It may be more expensive when you buy it, but it will save you money on power bills and helps the environment.

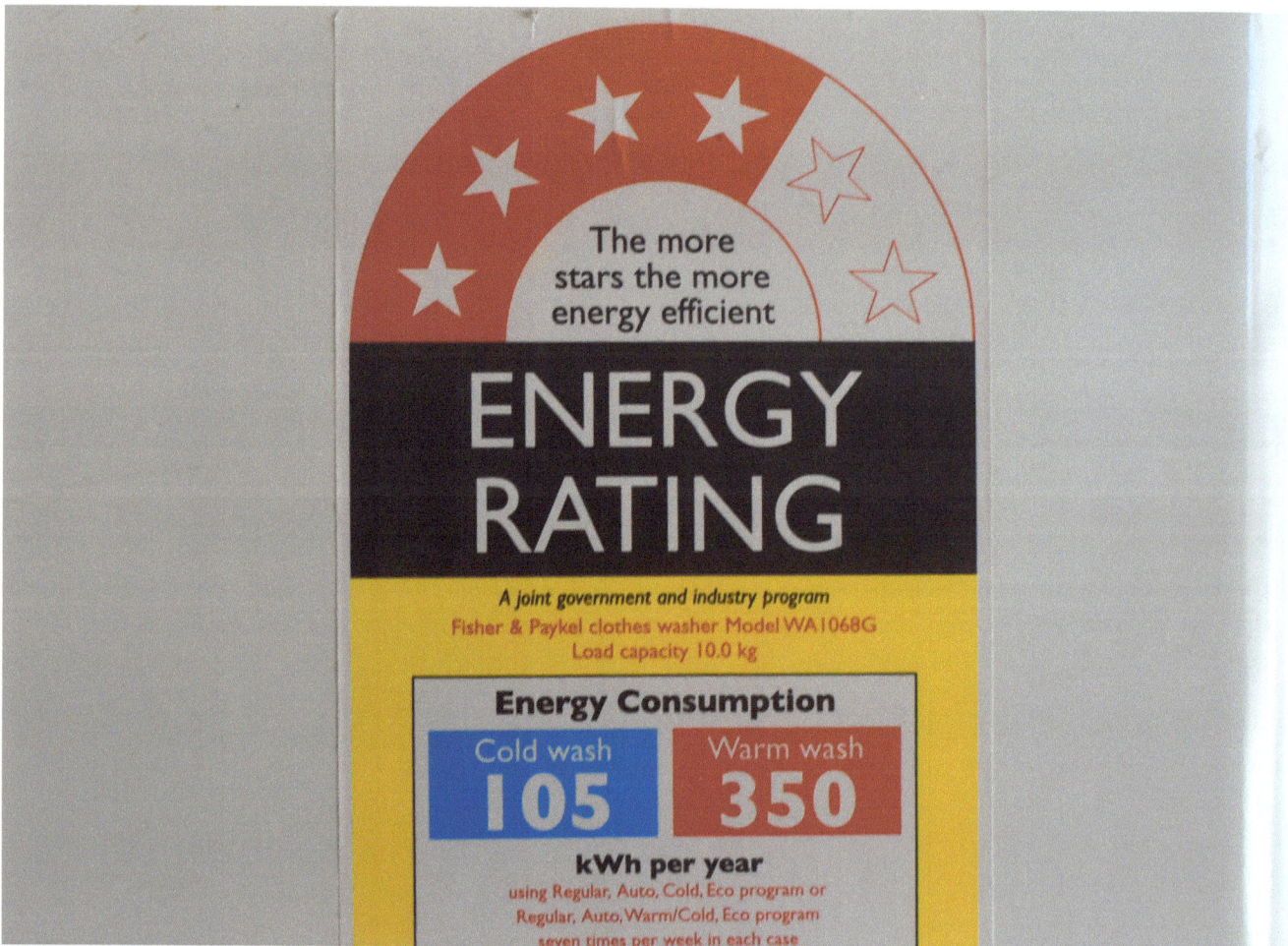

The more stars the more energy efficient

ENERGY RATING

A joint government and industry program
Fisher & Paykel clothes washer Model WA1068G
Load capacity 10.0 kg

Energy Consumption

Cold wash	Warm wash
105	350

kWh per year
using Regular, Auto, Cold, Eco program or
Regular, Auto, Warm/Cold, Eco program
seven times per week in each case

USE THE WASHING LINE INSTEAD OF THE DRYER

WHY: The dryer uses a lot of energy to produce the heat to dry your clothes. By using a washing line, clothes are dried using free solar energy and wind.

HOW: Use a washing line! If you don't like your clothes getting damaged by the sun, place the washing line in the shade, place shade over the washing line or use a drying rack inside the house. We put our clothes on the washing line late in the afternoon, overnight or early morning so they have minimal time in direct sunlight.

WAYS TO BE ENERGY EFFICIENT

INVEST IN SOLAR PANELS IF YOU ARE ABLE

WHY: Solar technology has become readily accessible and affordable to every household. Energy from the sun is free and solar power only requires an initial cost for supply and installation. By using solar energy you reduce your usage of power provided by environmentally unfriendly means such as coal and diesel.

HOW: Research commercial solar panel providers to determine which package is right for you. You will help the environment and your power bills. We have solar panels on the roof of our shed which provides most of our power needs. We also have solar powered lights around the house and solar powered torches. Some people have solar hot water systems that provide hot water to their house and some people have water pipe systems on the roof of their house which heats the water for their pool. Some people have solar panels to power electric fences and run small pumps on water bores.

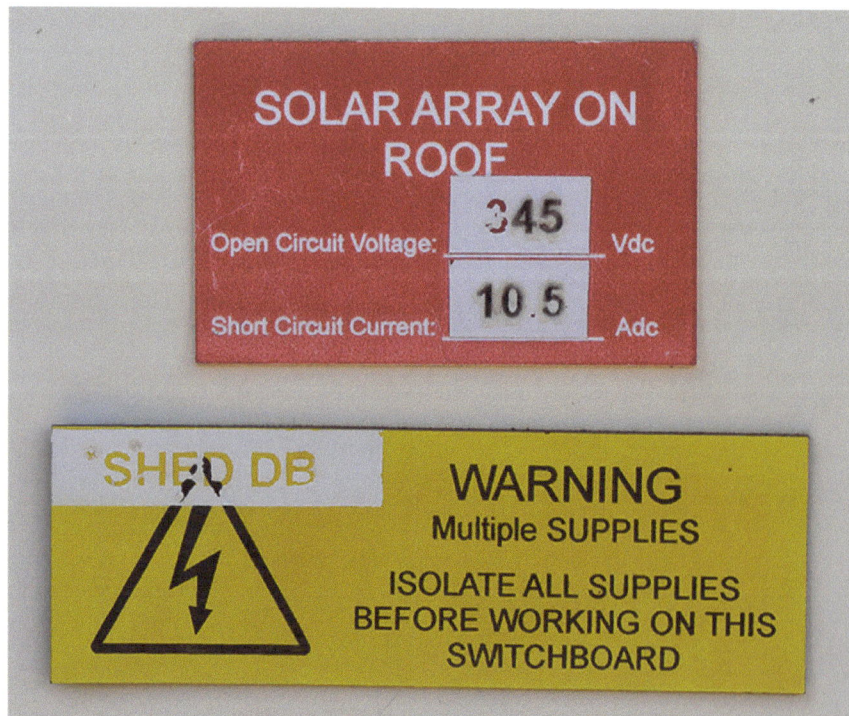

SOLAR ARRAY ON ROOF

Open Circuit Voltage: 345 Vdc

Short Circuit Current: 10.5 Adc

SHED DB

WARNING
Multiple SUPPLIES

ISOLATE ALL SUPPLIES
BEFORE WORKING ON THIS
SWITCHBOARD

WAYS TO BE TRANSPORT EFFICIENT

TRY WALKING TO SCHOOL

WHY: Going to school in a car uses fuel. Any other way of getting to school will help the environment, help you be healthier and save you money.

HOW: We know in the Goldfields that sometimes it is just too hot to walk home from school! But even walking or riding to school some of the time through the school year can help reduce fuel usage. If walking isn't your thing, you can use a scooter, bicycle, skates or even a horse!

CONSIDER INVESTING IN AN ELECTRIC CAR

WHY: New advances in car technology happen all the time. Keep up to date with cars that can save you fuel and money by being more efficient.

HOW: Electric cars are a relatively new addition to our roads. They are environmentally friendly and will play a bigger role in our community in the future. Think about the type of car you have – larger cars can be useful but use a lot more fuel and cost a lot more to run. We have a 4wd for work and offroad use and a smaller car which uses less fuel to run around town in.

Image by Paul Brennan from Pixabay

TRANSPORT

Most of the cars in Kalgoorlie are powered either by diesel or petrol. By burning these fuels it creates pollution and greenhouse gases which contributes to global warming. To be more sustainable, try to invest in an electric car or use public transport such as buses and trains. Maybe catch a lift with friends, ride a bike or walk to the places you need to go. Some fuels are more sustainable than others and different types of cars are more efficient than others. Think about what car your family drives, how often you use it and what you could do to be more sustainable on the roads.

WAYS TO BE SUSTAINABLE IN YOUR GARDEN

PLANT NATIVE PLANTS

WHY: Native plants have adapted to the soils, rainfall and climate of your area. They will be easier to look after and will provide a habitat for native animals as well.

HOW: We have selected a variety of native plants for our front yard that have beautiful flowers and colours in the bark and foliage. Shrubs, groundcovers and trees are thoughtfully placed to provide shade, protection or privacy. They also feed the native birds and insects which in turn provides a habitat for other animals such as reptiles.

GROW YOUR OWN FRUIT AND VEGETABLES

WHY: Maintaining a garden takes time and money. Why not grow plants that give you something in return, like fruit and vegetables? This is especially important in the dry Goldfields region, where water is precious, so try growing fruit trees which in return give you delicious fruit to eat.

HOW: Take a good look at your garden and decide which fruit and vegetable plants will grow in different areas of your garden. Prepare the ground as needed and maintain the garden with water and fertilizer as you would normally. Enjoy the fruit and vegetables you can grow!

GARDENING

In Kalgoorlie, there are a lot of trees and plants that are not native to the area. This can affect local wildlife as they have adapted to the native trees and shrubs and have no use for non-native plants such as the palm tree. Native plants in your garden require less water and fertilizer and will provide food and shelter for native birds, reptiles and insects.

WAYS TO BE SUSTAINABLE IN YOUR GARDEN

IF YOU HAVE ANIMALS, SUCH AS CHICKENS OR HORSES, USE THE MANURE TO FERTILISE YOUR GARDEN

WHY: Fertilising your garden is a normal part of maintaining it. These can be expensive from gardening stores, but you can supplement these with natural fertiliser from your backyard.

HOW: If you have animals in your backyard, such as chickens, collect their manure to make your own fertilizer. We compost the chicken manure with hay and manure from the horses and blend it into the vegetable garden before planting with vegetable seedlings. The food waste we can't feed to our animals also gets blended into the compost.

USE SHADE CLOTHS OVER YOUR VEGETABLE GARDENS TO REDUCE WATER EVAPORATION AND KEEP THE GROUND COOLER

WHY: Shade cloths help in the hot summer months help to keep the ground cooler and help prevent the leaves from scorching. The cooler ground then has less evaporation.

HOW: We place a shade cloth over our vegetable garden from October through to March. Our other vegetable beds are shaded naturally from the harsh afternoon sun by shade from the nearby Eucalypt trees.

PETS

Lots of people have pets at home like dogs, chickens and cats. Pets are kept as companions or can work, like guide dogs, guard dogs and farm dogs. Pets are also kept as a source of food, giving us eggs, milk or meat. The number of pets that you have often depends on the amount or room you have at your house, the time you have to spend with them and the cost of keeping them.

Here are some ways we are sustainable with our pets.

SOME PETS GIVE US FOOD

WHY: Many people have pets for companionship or compassion. Why not gain something from your companion, such as eggs from chickens or ducks or milk from cows or goats?

HOW: You may not have room for a cow or goat, but most people have the room to keep a few chickens. We love fresh eggs every day and our chickens go to school for other kids to learn and enjoy. We use clean old hay which the horses don't eat, to line the chickens' nesting boxes. You could also use shredded waste paper. The boxes are made from recycled old containers such as milk crates and rubbish bins.

SOME PETS ARE USEFUL

WHY: Apart from keeping us company and providing us with food and manure, pets can be useful in other ways. They can help prevent the spread of pests such as fruitfly or guard our house from intruders.

HOW: Let your chickens or ducks into areas with fruit trees. They will eat the fallen fruit and other insects in the soil and mulch helping to prevent fruitfly and other plant diseases. They will also eat unwanted weeds and insects such as snails and slaters. Our dog, Dusty helps to protect our house by licking anyone who comes into the yard. Dusty also chases the crows away from our backyard when they come to pinch our chicken eggs.

WAYS TO BE SUSTAINABLE WITH PETS

YOU CAN FEED PETS YOUR FOOD WASTE

WHY: We all throw rubbish in the bins every day. Some of that rubbish is food waste. Give the food waste to your pets instead of filling the rubbish bins.

HOW: We have 4 food waste bins in our house.

We keep corn husks, carrots and apples for our horses. They also eat the plants of cauliflower and broccoli after we have cut the heads off for ourselves to eat. The Goldfields is very dry and there are no grassy paddocks for our horses. Sometimes we let the horses graze for a short time on our back lawn and when it does rain, we collect clean grass from the street verges and drains to give to them.

Any meat waste we keep for our dog.

All our other food waste goes to our chickens except for a couple of things they won't eat, like orange peel and teabags, which then goes into our compost bin to be returned to the vegetable garden.

Our friends give us waste for our chickens and we give them eggs in return. Sometimes we get fruit waste from the local school.

Don't forget the waste from your pets (manure) can then be used to grow more vegetables in your garden.

WAYS TO BE SUSTAINABLE AT HOME

USE ENERGY EFFICIENT WHITE GOODS (WASHING MACHINES, DRIERS, FRIDGES, KETTLES ETC).

WHY: Like other household appliances, look for energy efficient brands that help reduce your power bill and also use less power.

HOW: Shop around for appliances in your house that suit your needs, have a good energy rating and put them in places that use minimum energy. For example, don't leave your fridge on your back veranda in the sun – it will use more energy than if it were in the shade.

USE YOUR APPLIANCES WISELY

WHY: Use appliances only when you need to helping to reduce your power bill and also to use less power.

HOW: Only use your air conditioner or heater when you need them and turn them off when you are not in the house. Use appliances such as the dishwasher or washing machine when they are full – they may adjust the water level but they use the same amount of power.

As you can see on this energy rating, a warm wash on your washing machine uses more than 3 times the energy of a cold wash – so use a cold wash as much as possible

The more stars the more energy efficient

ENERGY RATING

A joint government and industry program
Fisher & Paykel clothes washer Model WA1068G
Load capacity 10.0 kg

Energy Consumption

Cold wash	Warm wash
105	350

kWh per year
using Regular, Auto, Cold, Eco program or
Regular, Auto, Warm/Cold, Eco program
seven times per week in each case

AT HOME

Over the years, architecture and the design of housing has changed to be more environmentally friendly. Designs such as double glazing, insulation and grey water systems are now standard in many houses.

WAYS TO BE SUSTAINABLE AT HOME

USE ENVIRONMENTALLY FRIENDLY CLEANING PRODUCTS

WHY: Environmentally friendly products contain less ingredients that are harmful to the environment such as phosphates. They also are biodegradable – that is they break down into harmless products more readily.

HOW: There is a large range of environmentally friendly cleaning products in the supermarkets to buy. You can also make your own cleaning products at home from natural ingredients such as lemon and vinegar. This can also be done in the garden by making natural pest control products using ingredients such as garlic, soap or oils.

SO MANY WAYS TO RECYCLE!

WHY: We all generate a lot of waste each day. A lot of that waste can be used again or recycled. By taking the time to separate recycled material from non-recyclable material we can reduce the amount of waste going to landfill, left in the environment or in the oceans.

HOW: Look around for recycling projects and stations. Most suburbs run a recycling bin collection alongside the traditional rubbish bin. Some suburbs have a third bin separating and recycling organic waste – that's food waste if you don't have chooks. You can claim money at recycling stations in some states for aluminium cans, plastic bottles and glass. There are also charities collecting recyclable material such as the Country Women's Association (CWA) in Kalgoorlie that collects plastic bread tags to raise money for wheelchairs in other countries. Aluminium ringpulls from bottles can be collected and used to make artificial limbs. Empty ink cartridges from printers can be recycled. Find out if your suburb has recycling projects available or encourage your local council to do so.

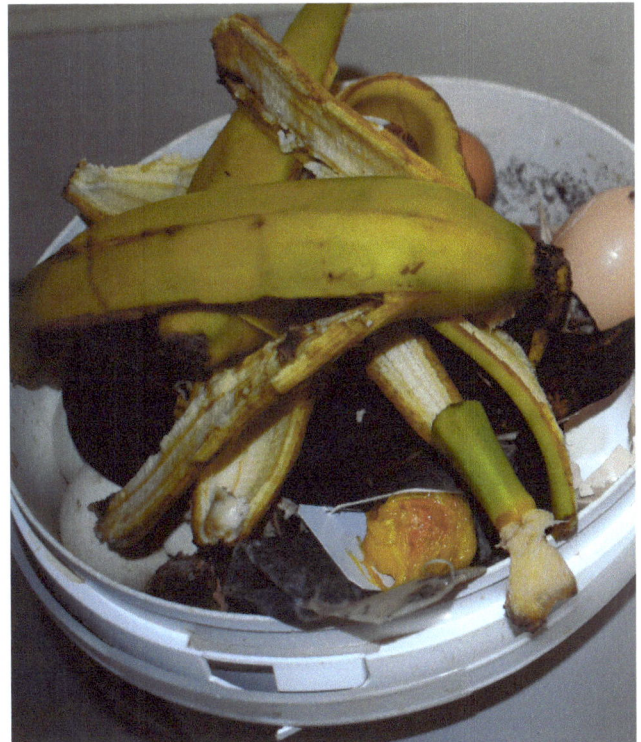

WAYS TO BE SUSTAINABLE AT HOME

RECYCLE GREY WATER

WHY: Recycling grey water helps to use less water.

HOW: There are professional grey water systems that can be included into the plans of new houses or added onto older houses. Or you could recycle your grey water yourself, like bucketing your bath water onto the garden or using a hose to let the washing machine water drain onto your lawn.

USE THE HALF & FULL FLUSH BUTTONS ON YOUR TOILET

WHY: Most modern houses have more than one toilet. A lot of water is used to flush away our waste so by using the appropriate button on the toilet you can save a lot of water over the year.

HOW: Most modern toilets have either a full or half flush button and everyone knows what they are for. Remember to use the correct button to help save a lot of water that is "wasted".

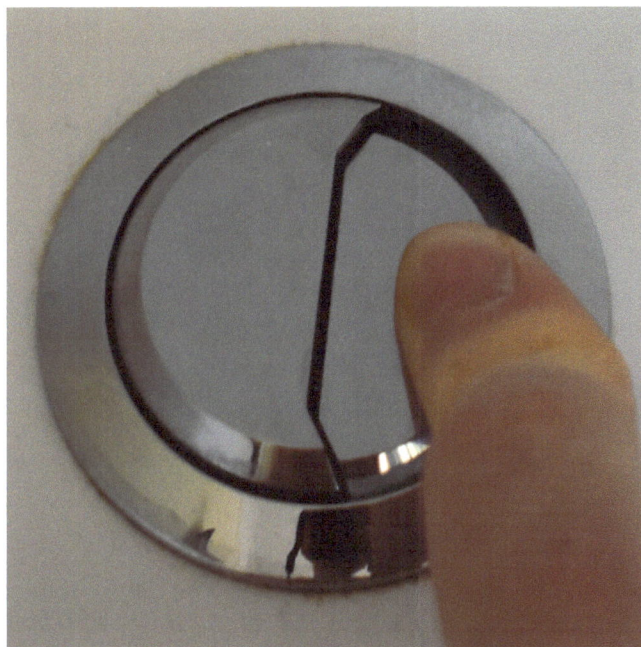

REDUCE YOUR SHOWER TIME TO CONSERVE WATER. TIMERS CAN HELP

WHY: Like the toilet, a lot of water is used to wash ourselves.

HOW: Consider how many showers you have – do you really need to shower as often as you do? How long do you spend in the shower – can you reduce the time? A small timer can help you judge the amount of time you spend in the shower. A small saving in shower time can add up to a lot of water at the end of the year.

WAYS TO BE SUSTAINABLE AT HOME

MAKE SURE YOUR TAPS DON'T LEAK

WHY: A constantly dripping tap can release a lot of water over time. A drip over 24 hrs could be several litres of water that turns into 100's of litres over the year.

HOW: Check over the taps to make sure they have been turned off without dripping. Fix any taps or shower heads that are leaking. That includes water pipelines running to the house from the front of the house and any reticulation lines in your garden. Check your water meter at the front of your house to see if it is running even when you have all water taps turned off around the house. If it is running, you could potentially have a leak you don't know about.

HEAT AND COOL ONLY THE ROOMS YOU NEED

WHY: Heating and cooling the house uses a large amount of energy. Only use these appliances when you need them. Try to heat or cool only the rooms you need to use.

HOW: Put a jumper on before you turn the heater on. Close up the house before you need to put the air conditioner on. Close the doors to unoccupied rooms so you only heat or cool the rooms you are using.

WAYS TO BE SUSTAINABLE AT HOME

WASTE FREE LUNCHBOX

WHY: Wrapping your lunch in plastic wrap or plastic bags creates a lot of plastic waste. If you buy food already pre-packaged, all the wrapping creates a lot of waste that goes to the tip.

HOW: Take your food to school in washable re-useable containers that can be used many times. You could also try wraps such as beeswax wraps. Instead of buying pre-packaged food like biscuits, buy a large bag and put portions into re-useable containers. Lunchtime food waste and scraps can be brought home for your poultry or compost if your school doesn't provide for waste food collection.

OTHER WAYS TO BE SUSTAINABLE

- Maybe your school can have a collection bin for food waste that could be given to poultry or composted for the vegetable garden.

- Do you know if your school recycles plastic and/or paper waste?

- What about printer ink cartridges? They can be recycled as well.

- Find out if your suburb has recycling projects available or encourage your local school or council to do so.

- Does your teacher only use the air conditioner when the classroom is being used? Are the lights turned off when no one is in the classroom?

- Don't forget to take reusable bags to the supermarket!

OTHER WAYS
TO BE SUSTAINABLE

We can be sustainable in many other places – not just at home. Think about how you get to school, what you do when you are there and how you get home at the end of the day.

What is your school doing to be more sustainable? Our school is trying to do lots!

Our primary school has a vegetable garden, collects rainwater from the roofs of the classrooms and uses solar panels to help produce power.

The school encourages the students to bring waste-free lunches by having "Waste free Wednesday".

Students are encouraged not to waste water in the toilets and the school provides safe places to keep bikes and scooters for the students who don't come to school in a car.

The school encourages various recycling projects. There are charities collecting recyclable materials, such as aluminum ring pulls from bottles to make artificial limbs. We collect the plastic tags from the bread we buy and take them to school. A member from the local Country Women's Association (CWA) then collects the tags from school and sends them to a central collection point where they are sold to raise money for wheelchairs. You may find charities in your suburb that recycle food from local businesses, such as the bakeries.

Waste paper is often shredded at school for privacy reasons. Did you know shredded paper makes perfect nesting material for chickens?

WAYS TO BE SUSTAINABLE INTO THE FUTURE

RECYCLING

WHY: There are limited resources like iron ore in the world and at some point in the future, they will run out. We will need to become much more efficient at recycling and reusing what we have already used.

HOW: Through more efficient recycling stations and more efficient recycling services.

Image by Else Kitap from Pixabay

SUSTAINABLE POPULATION

WHY: Many of the problems we face are created by an expanding population – there are too many people! Too many people create too much rubbish, use too much of the world's natural resources and take up too much space in the environment, squeezing out other species.

HOW: Talks between the countries of the world need to address population growth and decide what is a sustainable population level. How many people is too many? How many people can the Earth sustain? People need to continue to develop new ways to sustain more people.

INTO THE FUTURE

Over the years, architecture and the design of housing has changed to be more environmentally friendly. Designs such as double glazing, insulation and grey water systems are now standard in many houses. People's thoughts and attitudes have changed, for example more and more people are recycling waste. Communities and cities are changing too, with councils providing more services and incentives to recycle. As the population of the world grows, so does its demand for resources. We simply can't just get more, so we have to use what we do have more wisely and recycle what we have already used. So what do you think the future will be like?

ENERGY

WHY: Fossils fuels will run out one day. It took millions of years to create them in the first place, so we will need to look to other ways for our energy needs.

HOW: We think there will be more use of solar energy in the Goldfields Region. Solar farms producing electicity to power our homes. Solar farms to power industries. Solar panels on cars and lights. New technology to capture the energy created by water, wind and steam.

Image by D.Cannon from Pixabay

WAYS TO BE SUSTAINABLE INTO THE FUTURE

We think that recycling, energy production and a sustainable population will be the overall main focus of a sustainable future. As you have read in our book – sustainability can start right at home in your own backyard.

Our future backyard may be quite different to the way it is now. Capturing and storing rainwater, renewable energy production systems, recycling waste, food production and native gardens need to be a focus of future backyards if we are all to make a difference.

"from little things, big things grow"

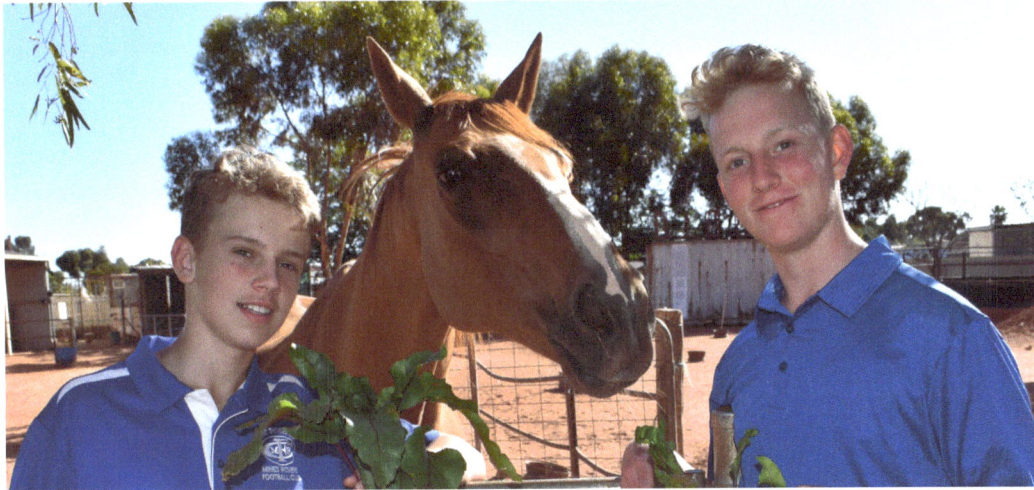

REFERENCES

How sustainable is sustainability? - Oxford College of Procurement and Supply. Retrieved
    26 September 2019, from https://www.oxfordcollegeofprocurementandsupply.com/
    how-sustainable-is-sustainability/

PHOTO CREDITS

All photos used in this book are family images or shot by Jared Campbell with the exception of the following copyright free images sourced from Pixabay and listed below:

Page 8   Image by Pexels from Pixabay

Page 12   Image by Paul Brennan from Pixabay

Page 34   Image by Elise Kitap from Pixabay

Page 35   Image by D.Cannon from Pixabay